This Book Belongs To

_____

_____

Copyright 2022 Acts 10.1 Books
Jobos101 is Trademarked by: Jahlyric Boldini Designs, Llc
www.Jobos101.com

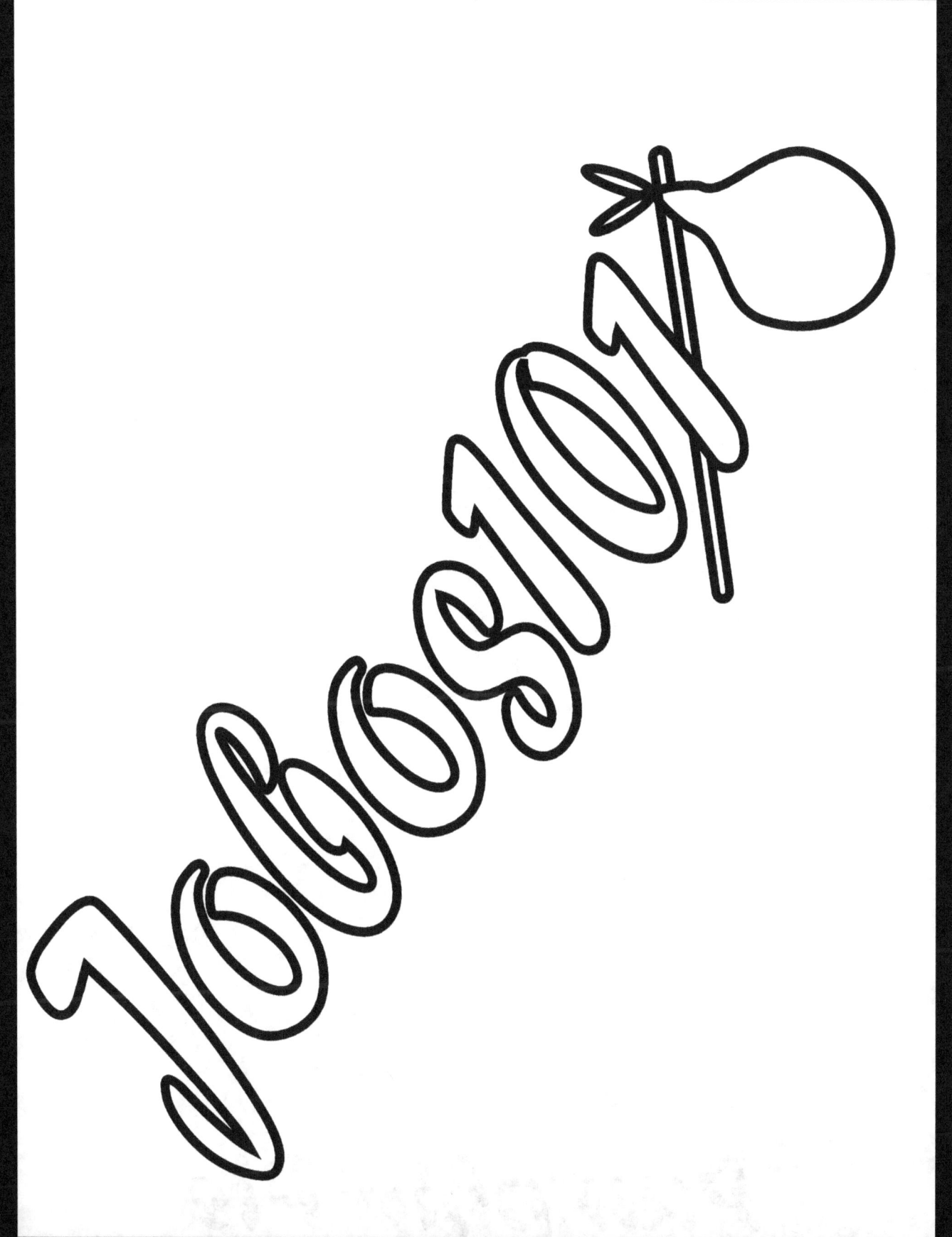

Pumpkin Pie

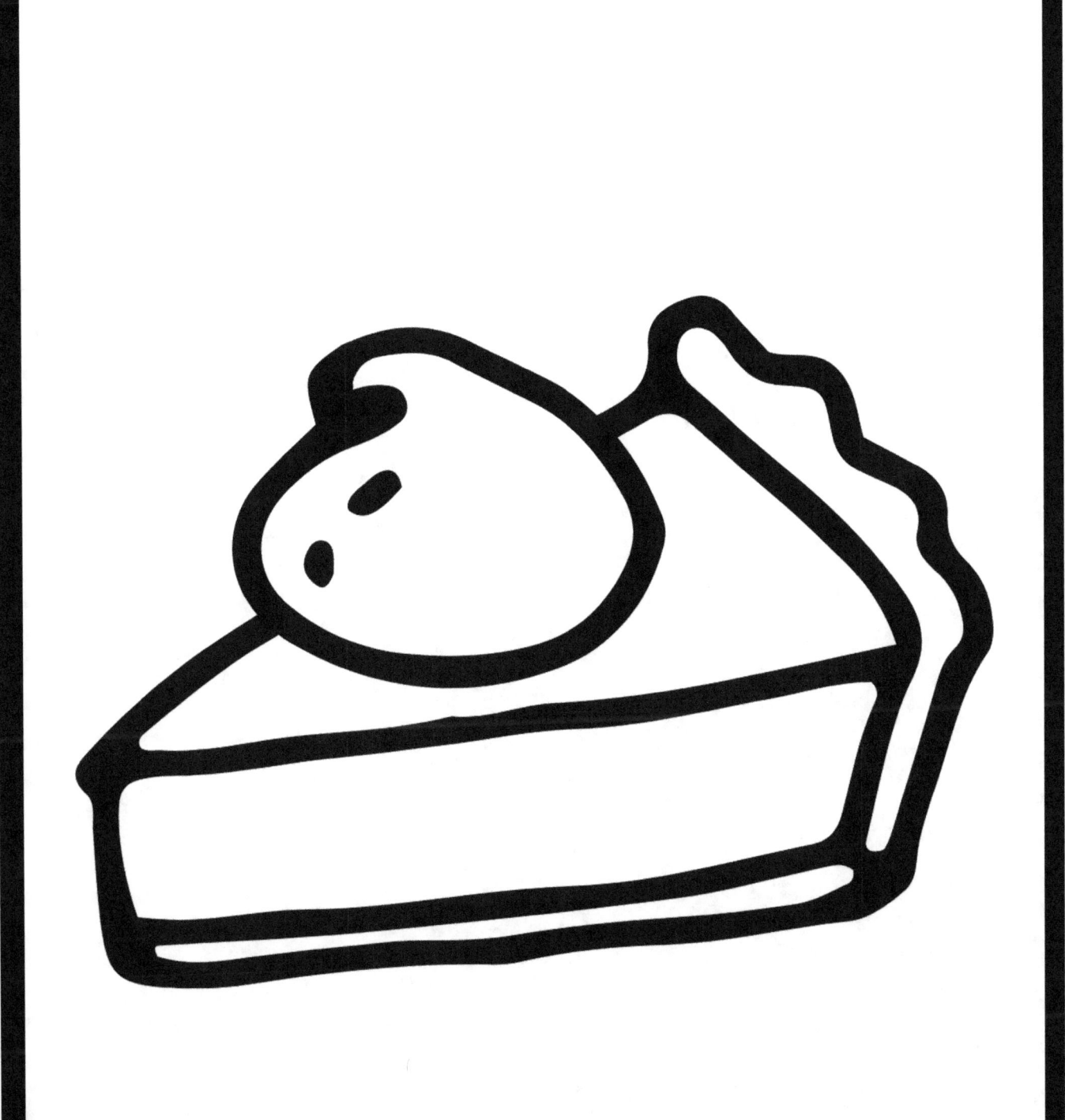

Coconut Cake

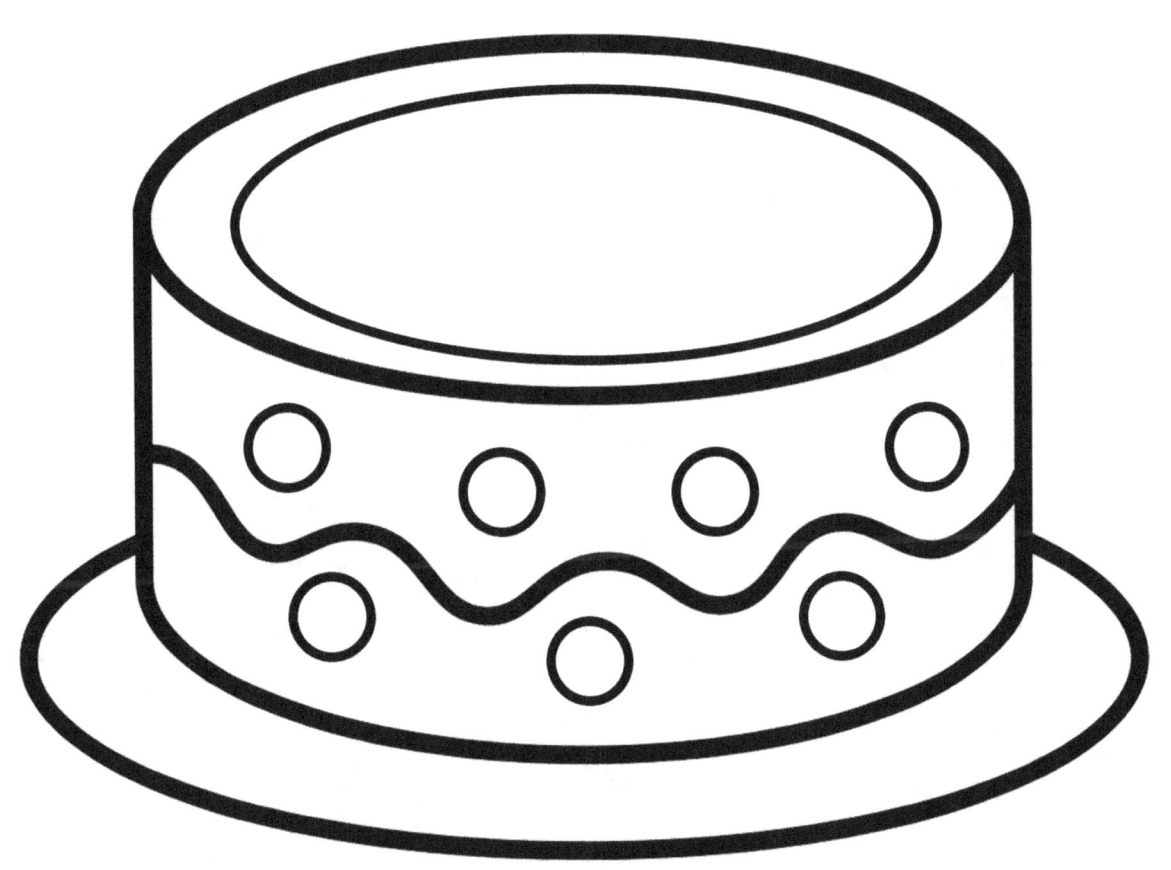

Whipcream Frosted Cake

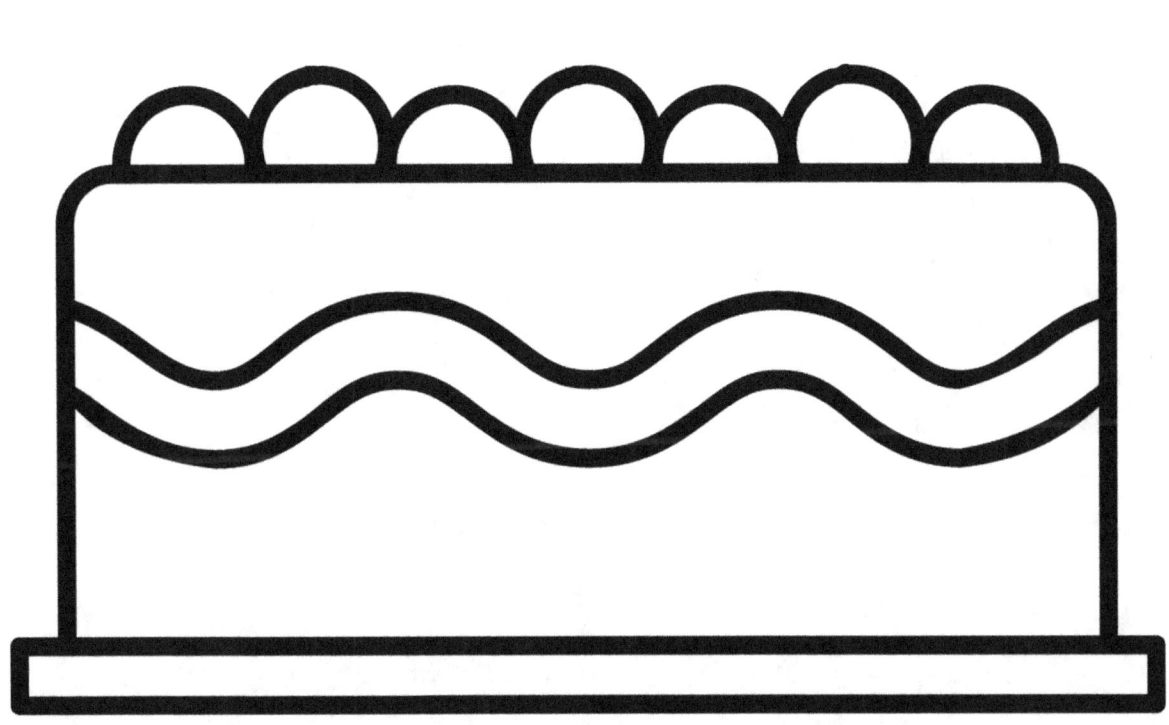

Apple Pie

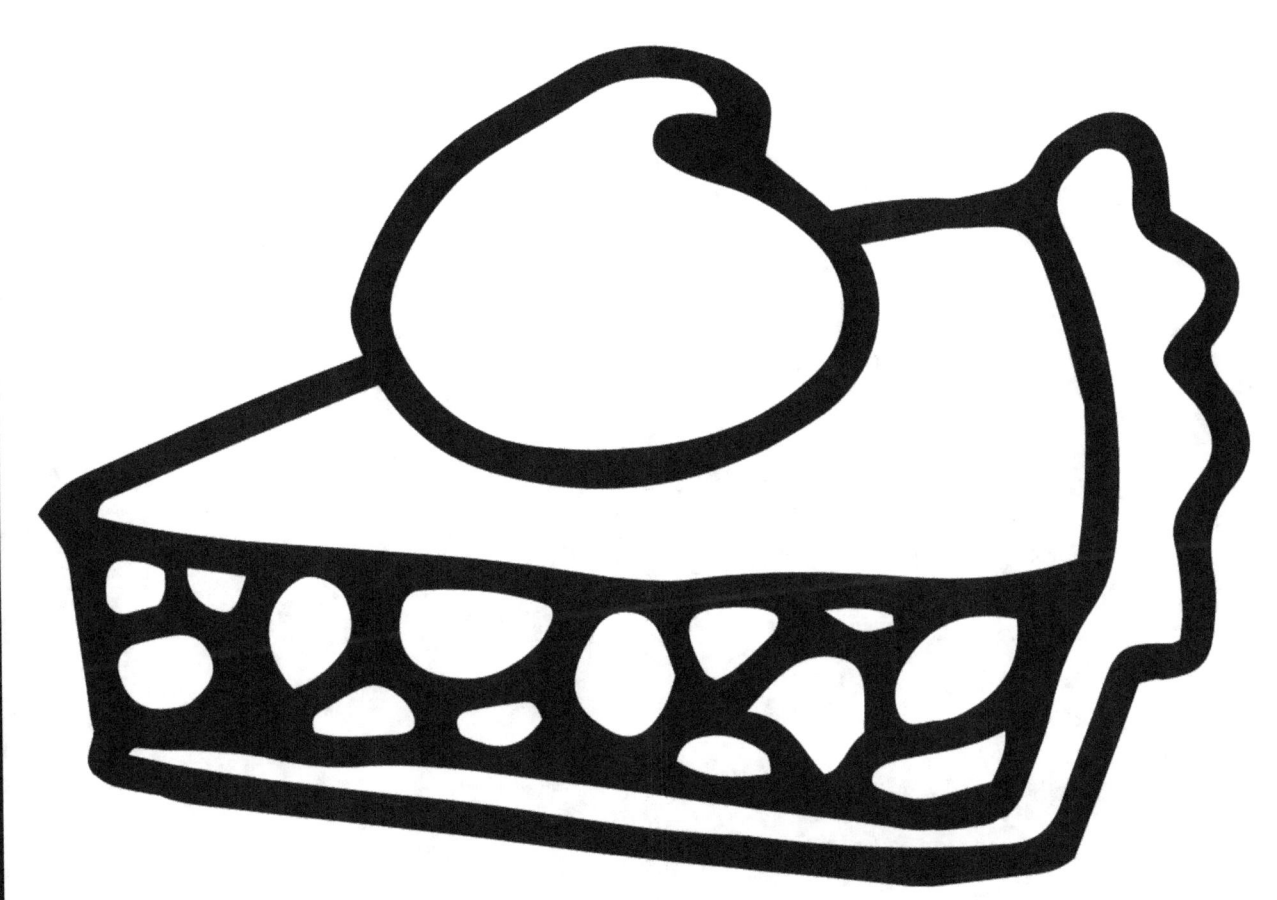

3 Scoops of Sherbert

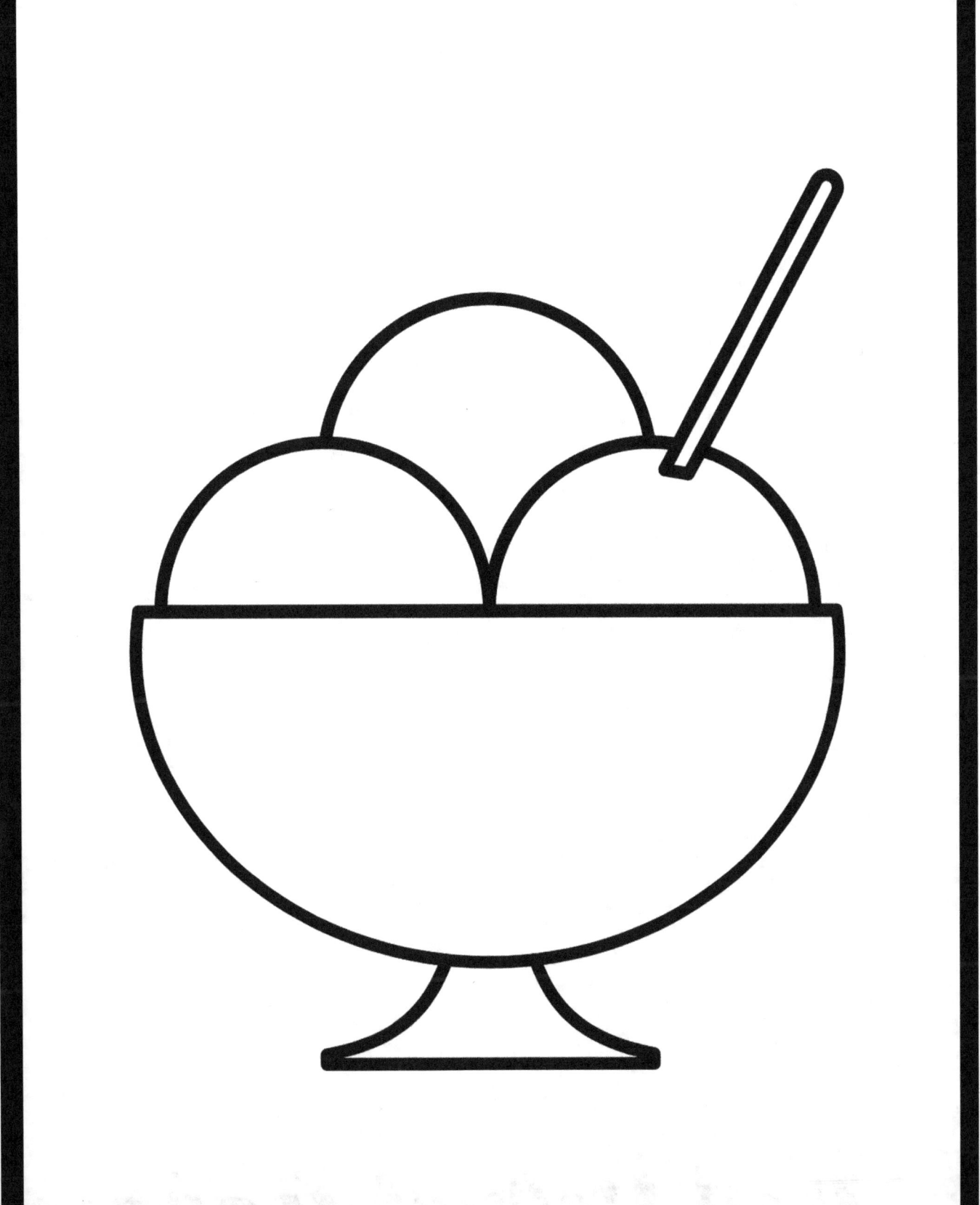

Red Velvet Cake

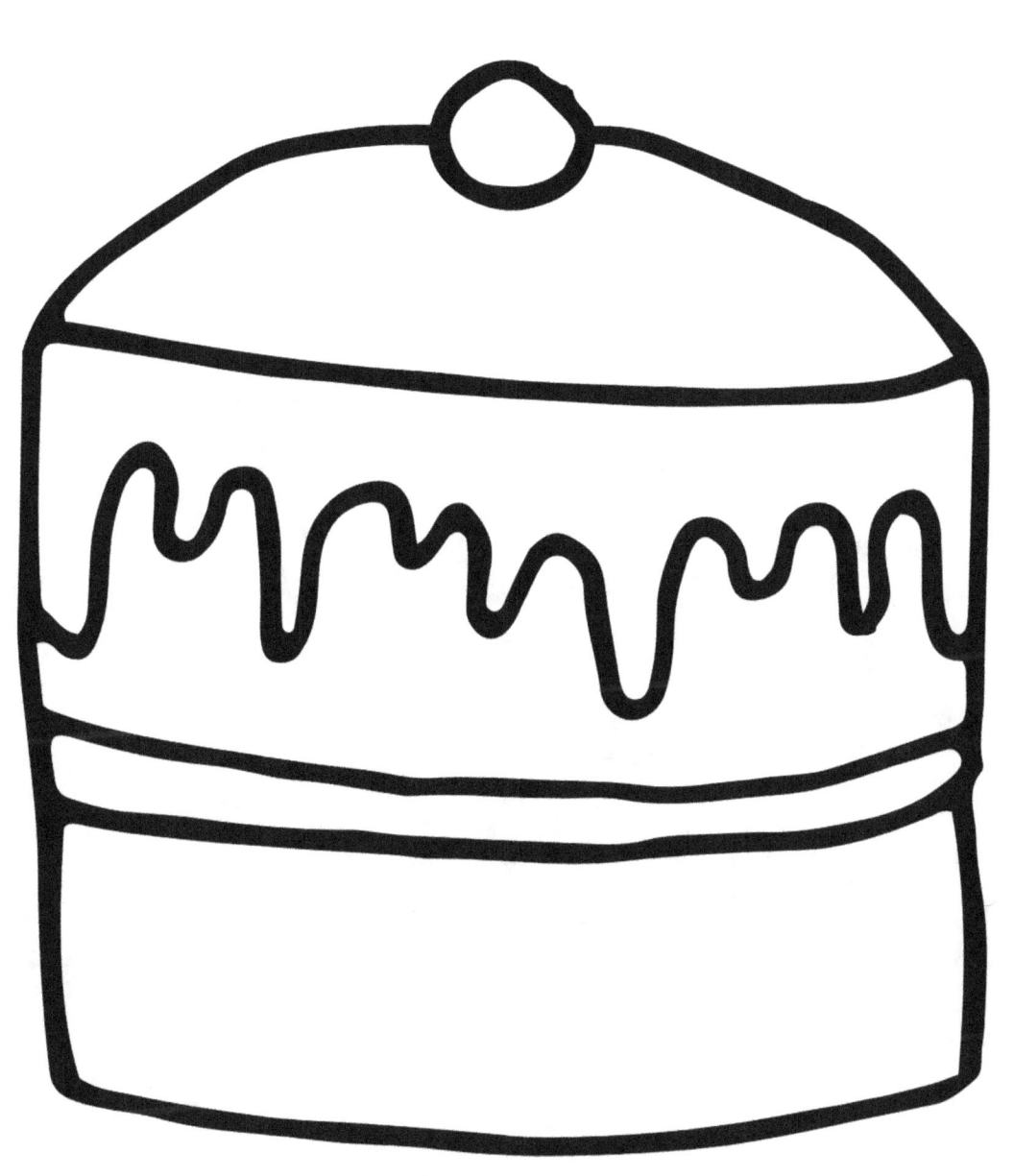

Cinamon Muffin

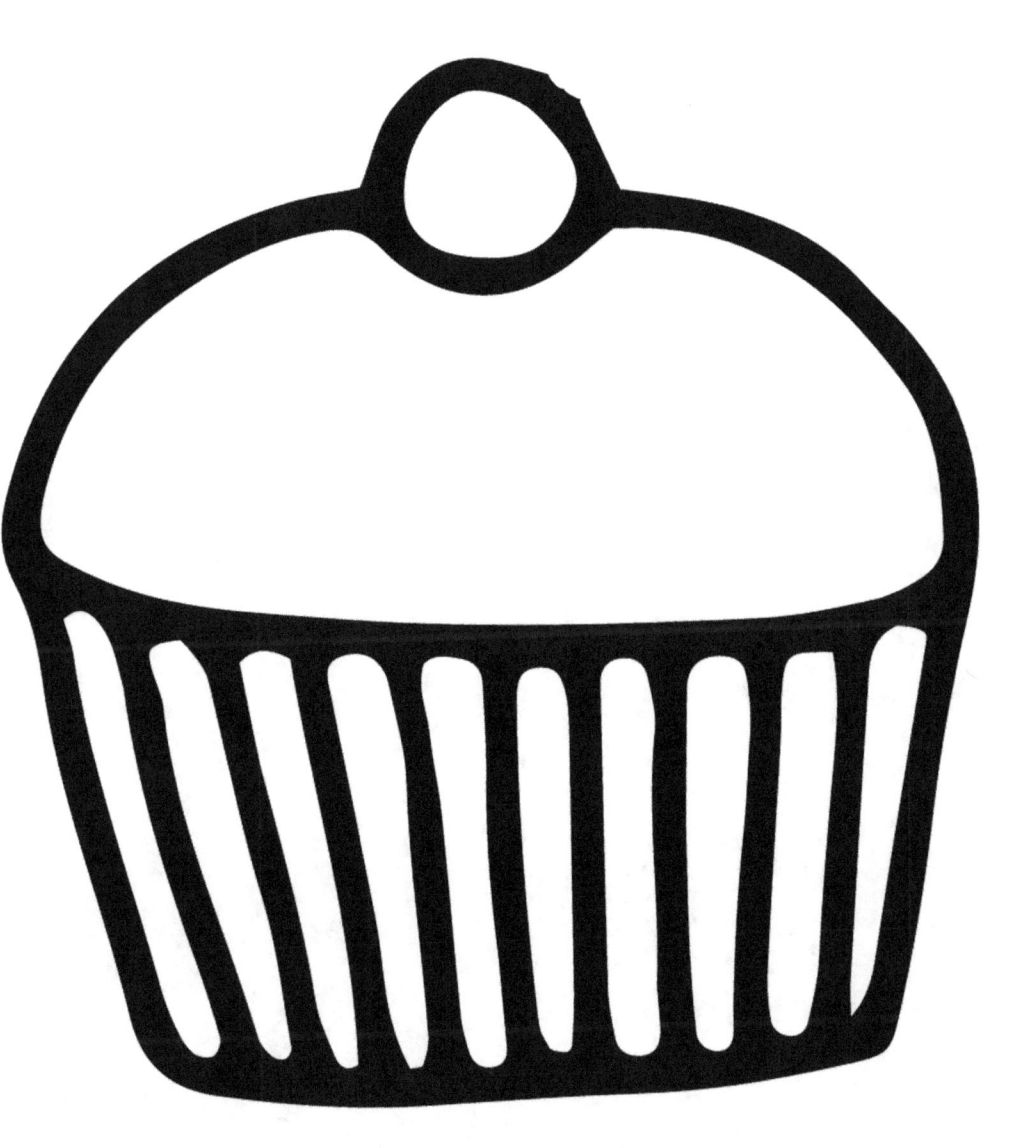

Sweet Potato Pie

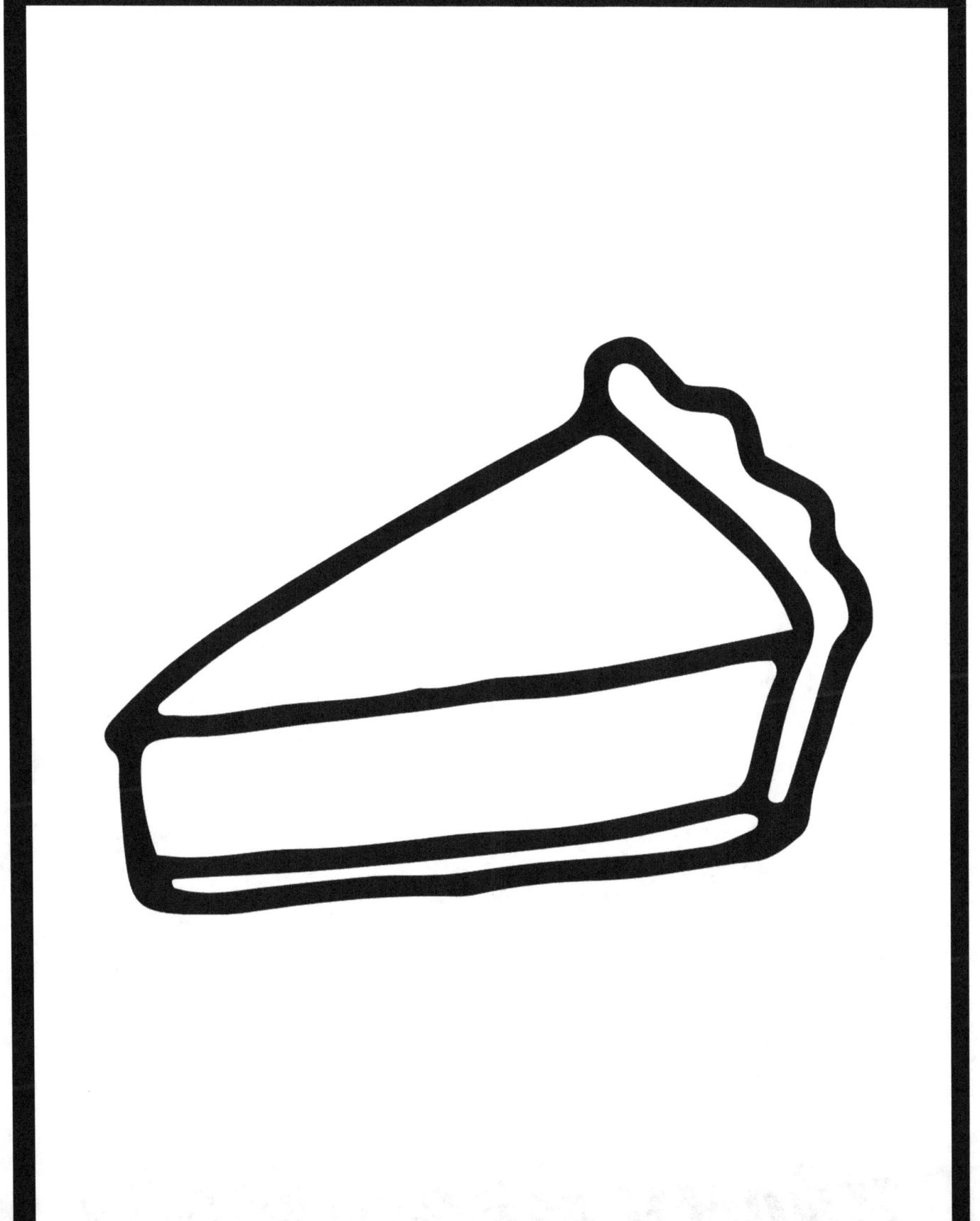

Cherry Cheesecake

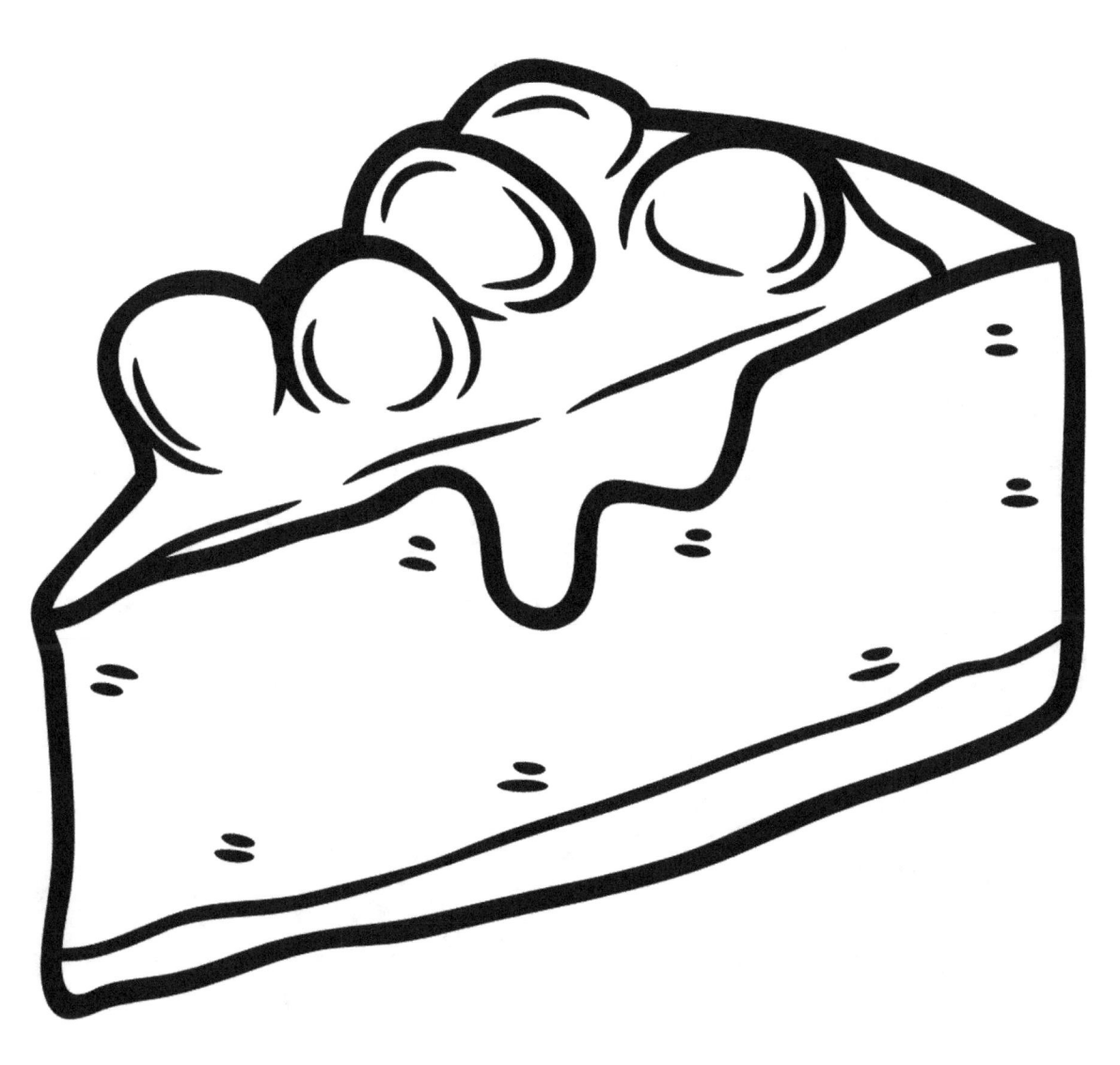

Dutch Apple Pie

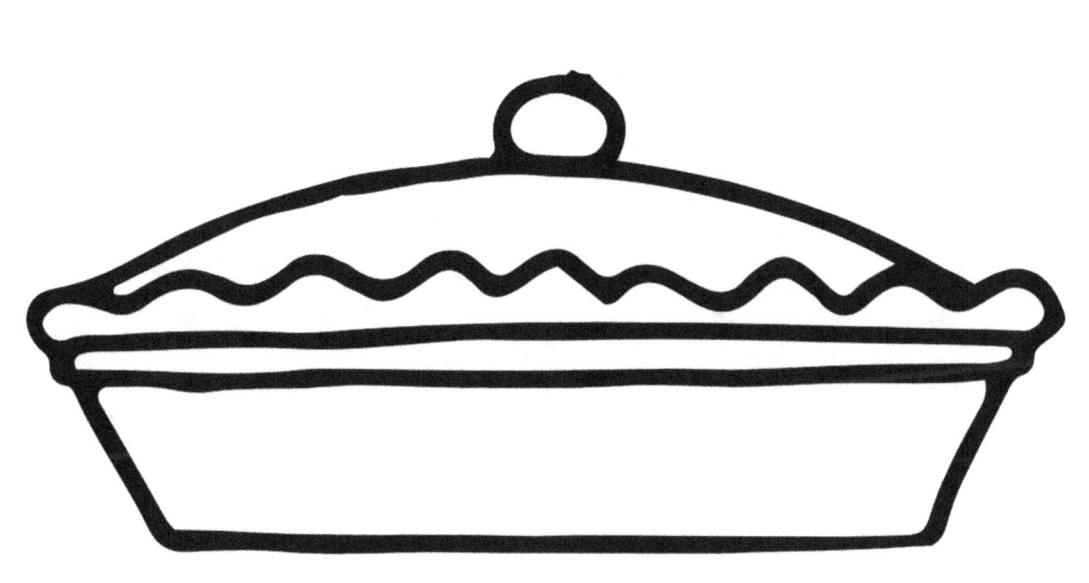

Limon Meringue Pie

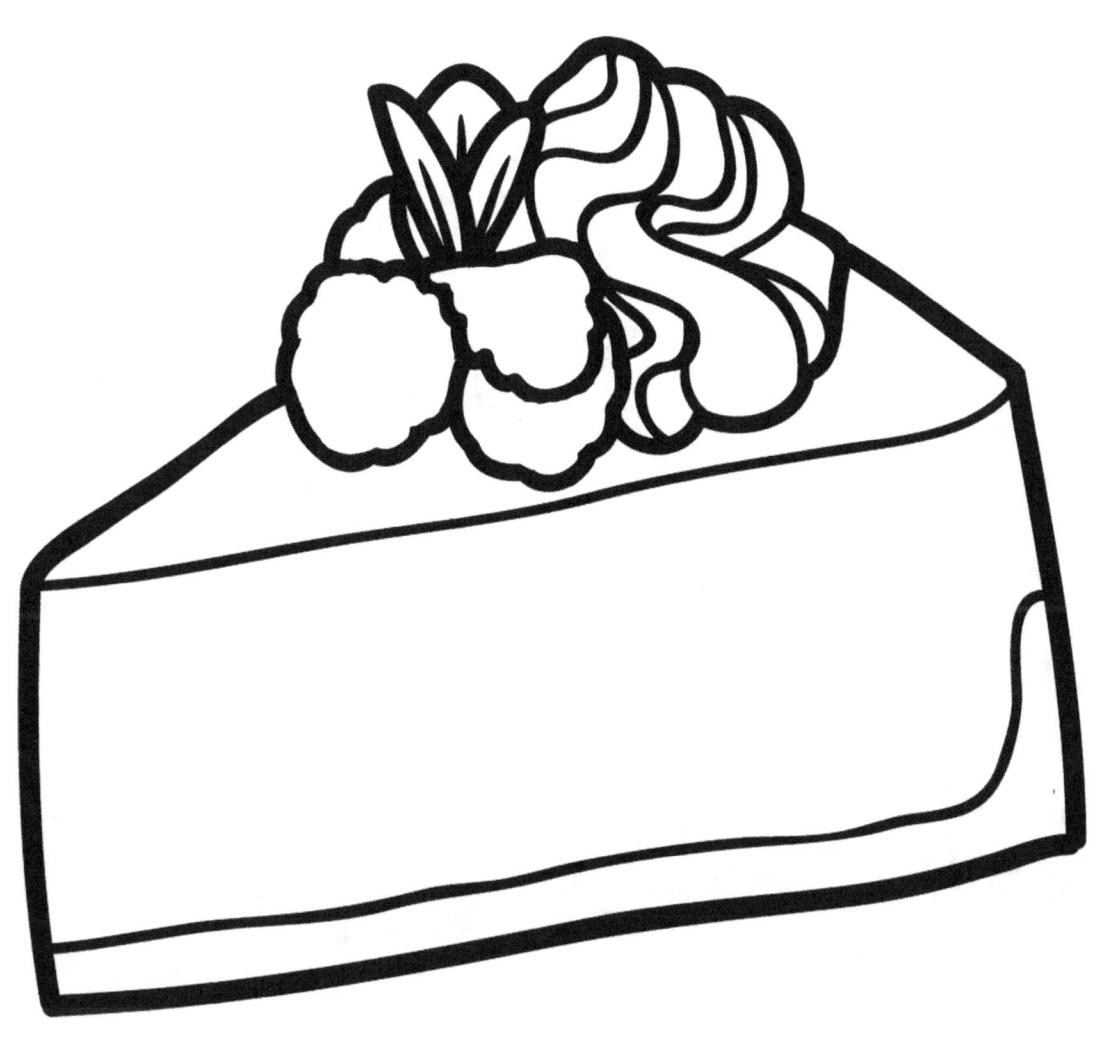

Chocolate Frosted Cake

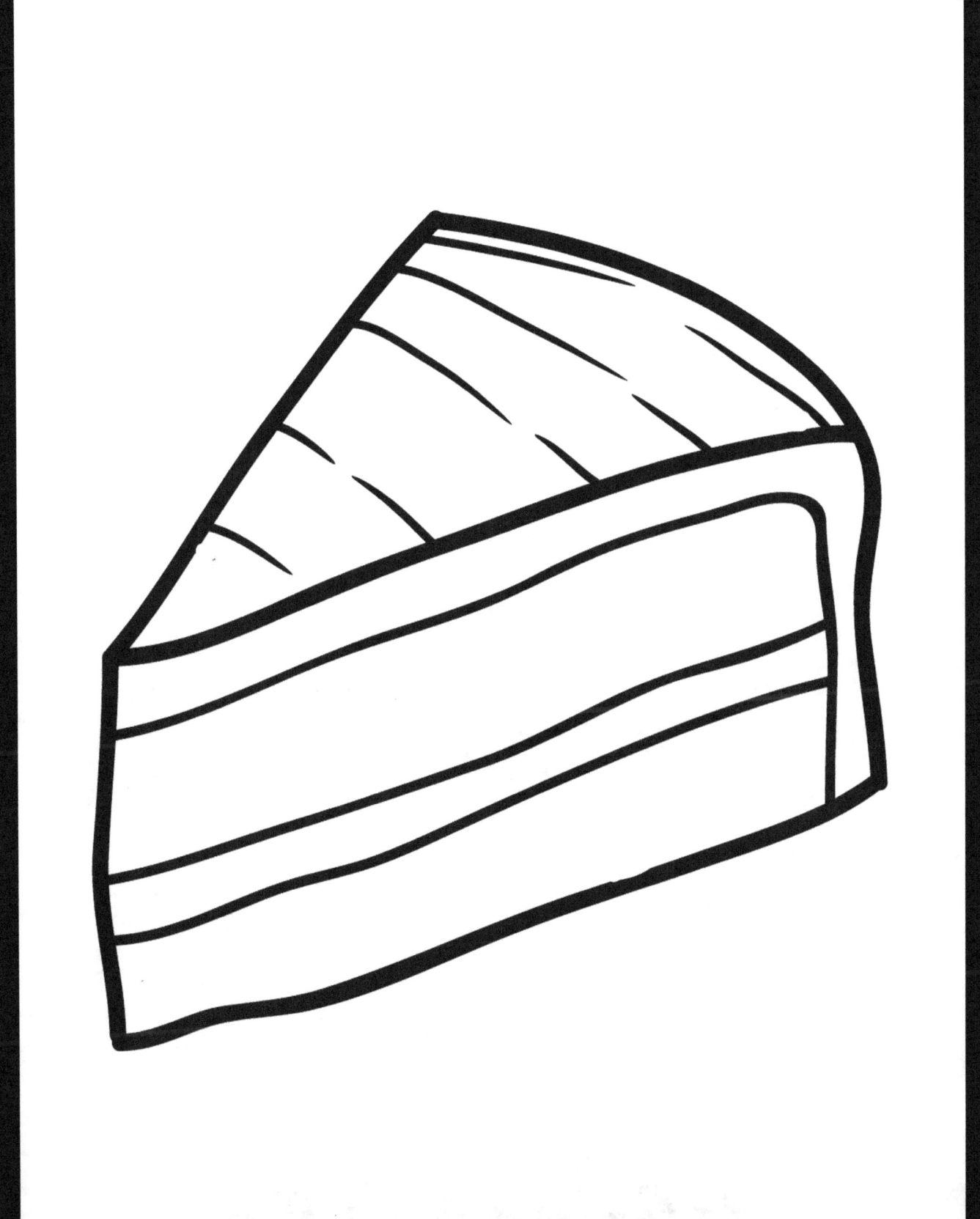

Cheesecake

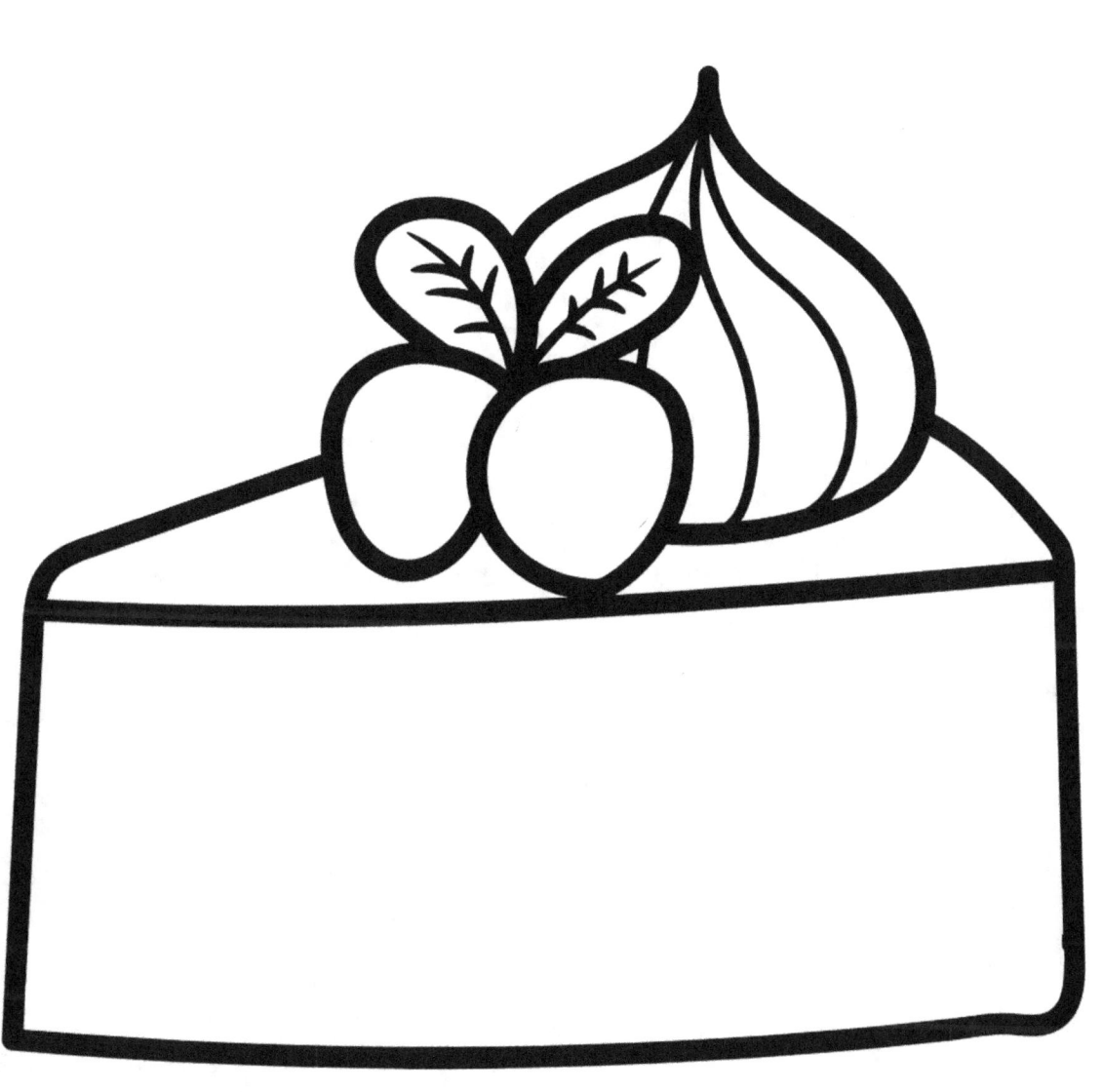

Fruit Cake

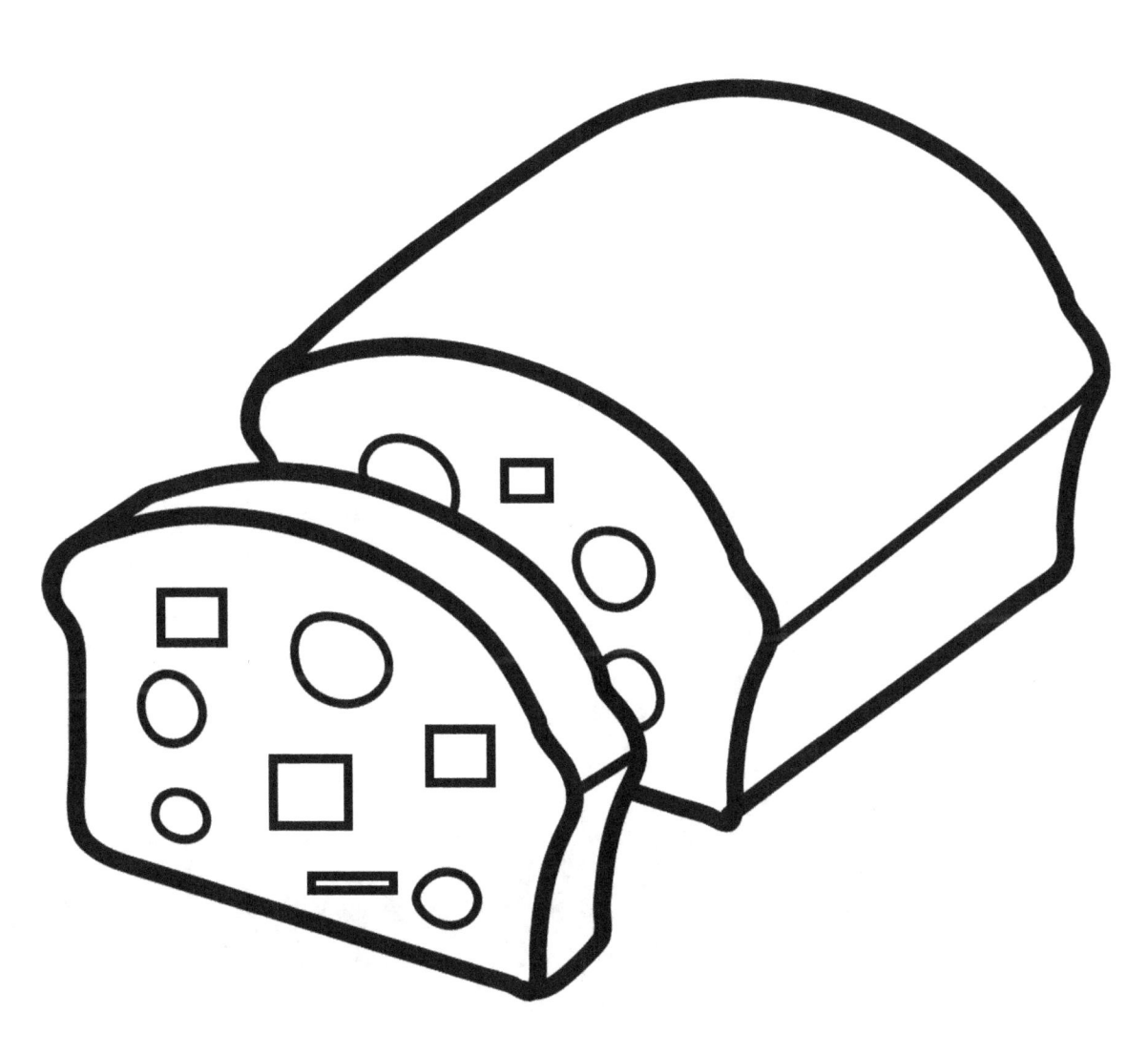

Banana Crunchcake

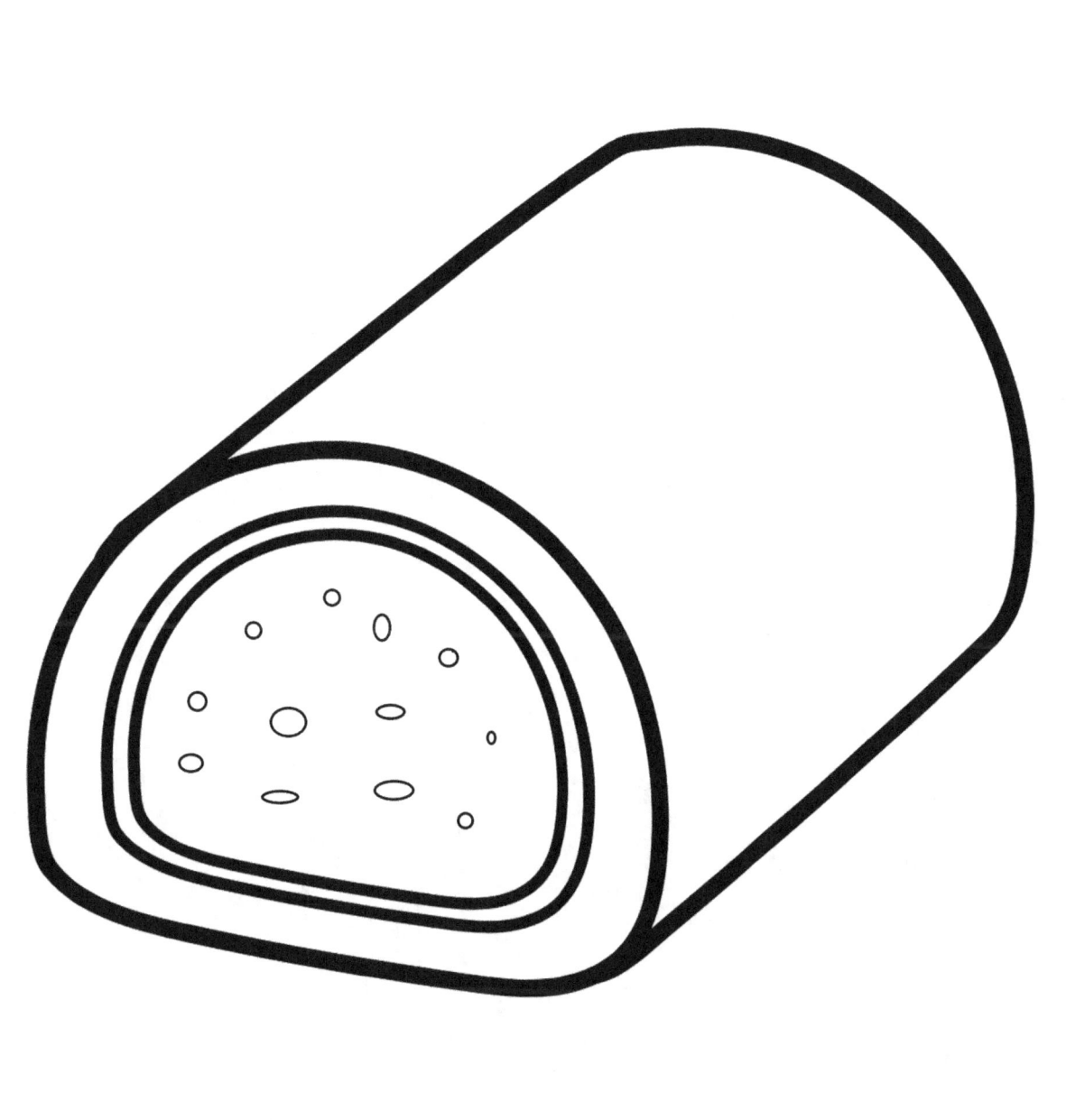

Vanilla Cupcake

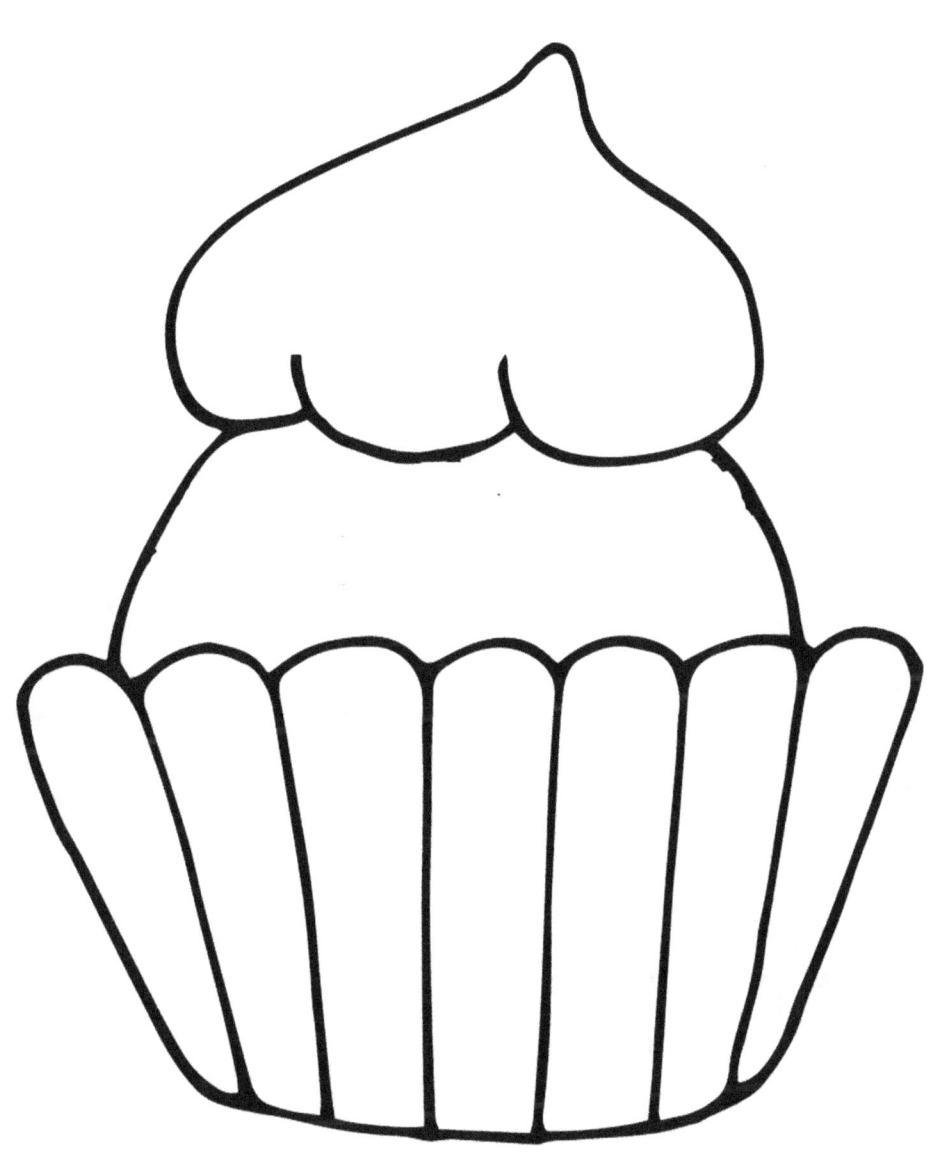

Strawberry Jelly Cake

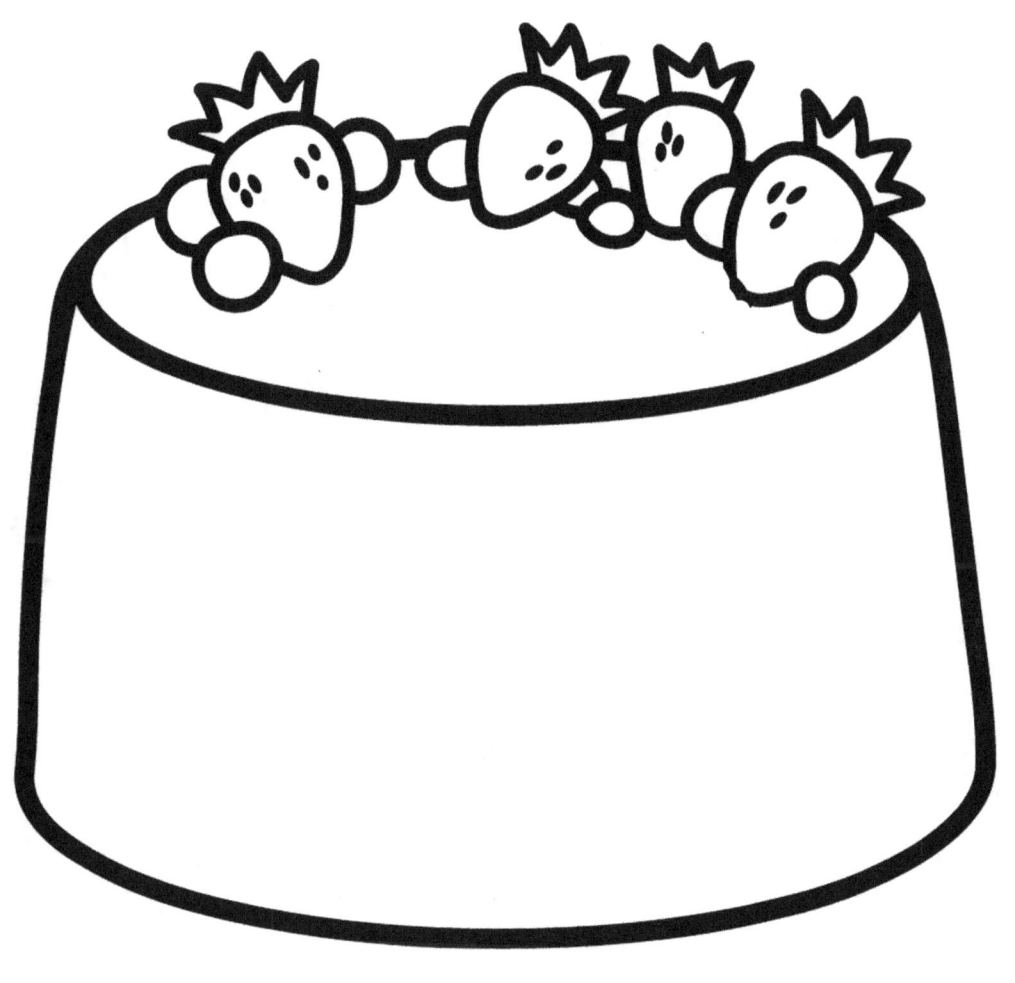

Fruit Topped Cake

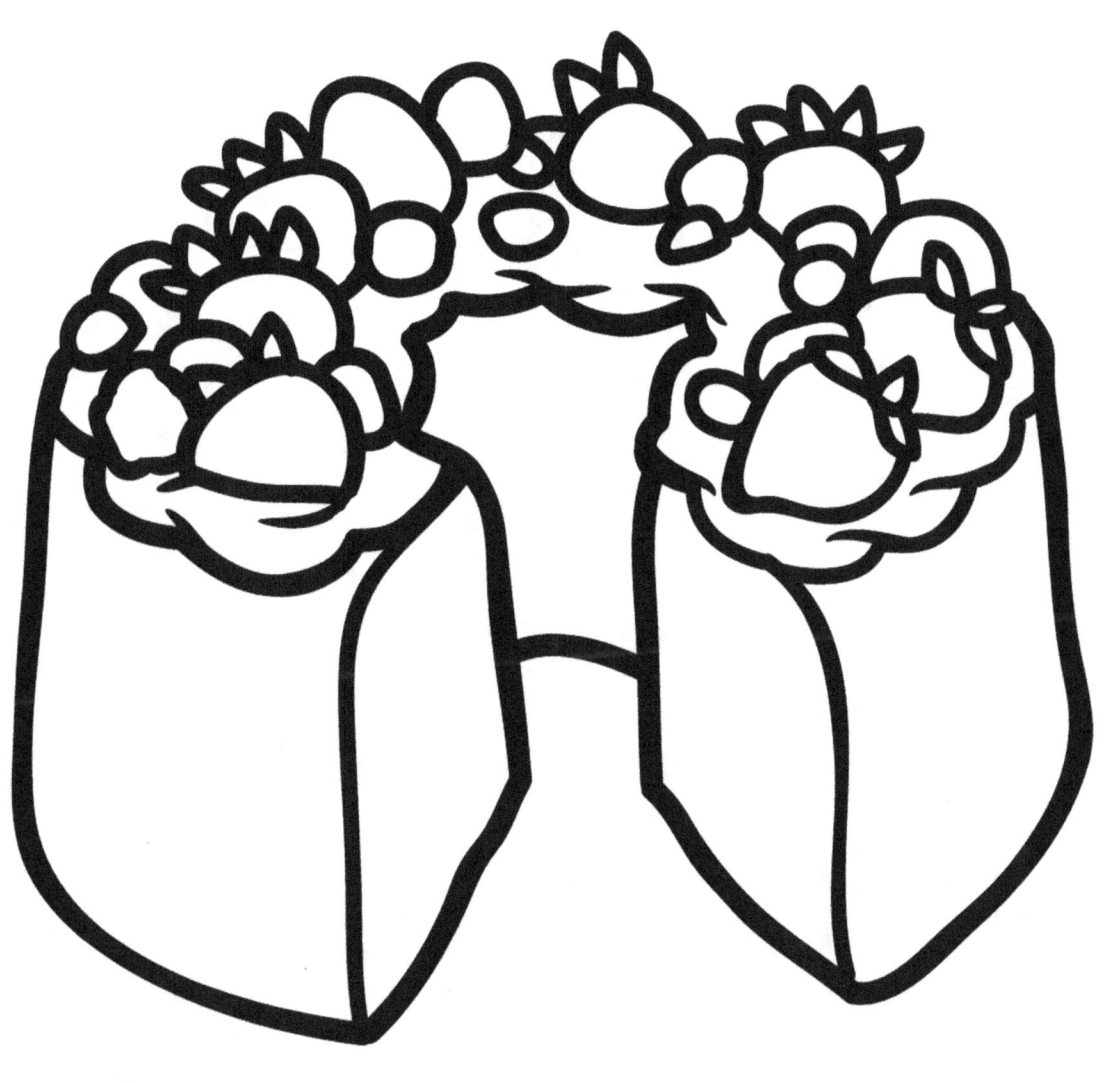

Lemon Poundcake

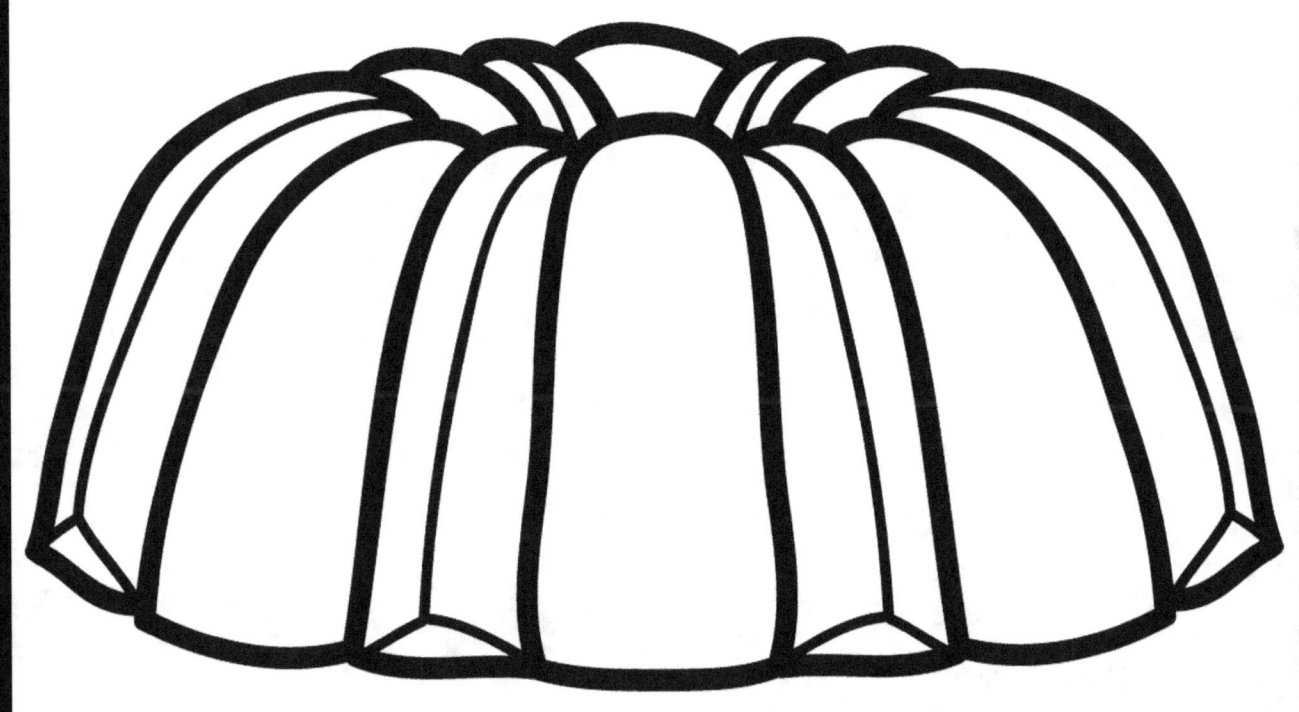

Soft Ice Cream Cone

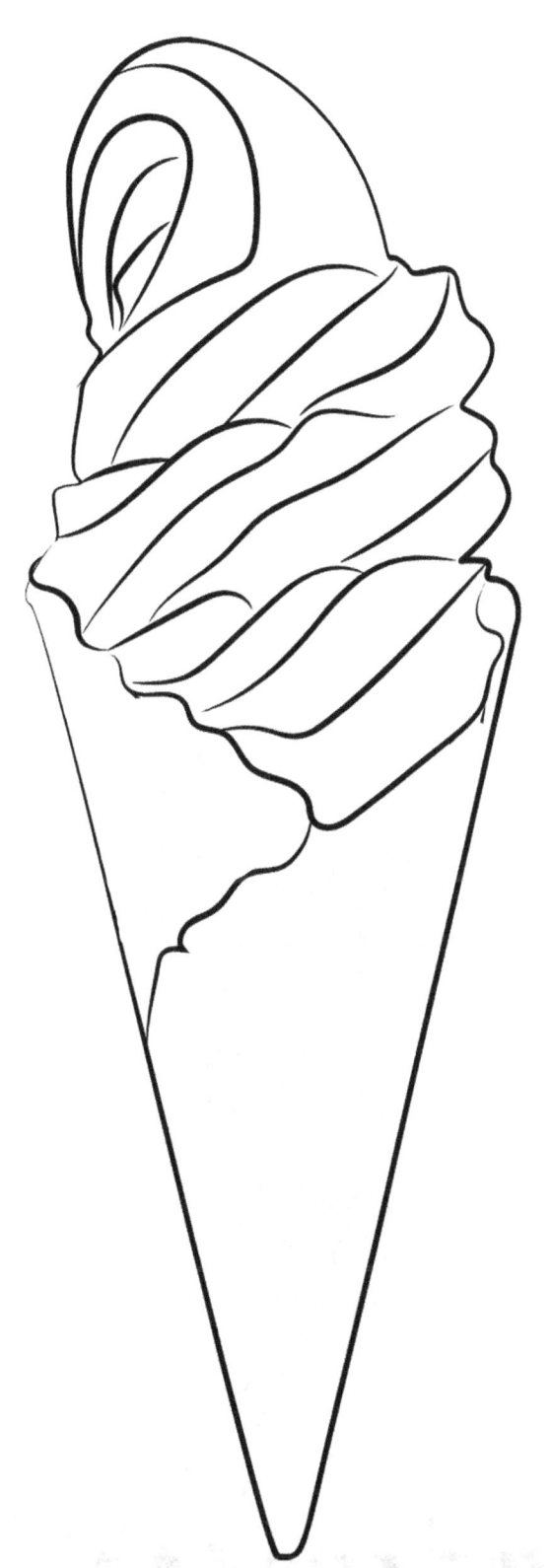

Swirl Waffle Cone

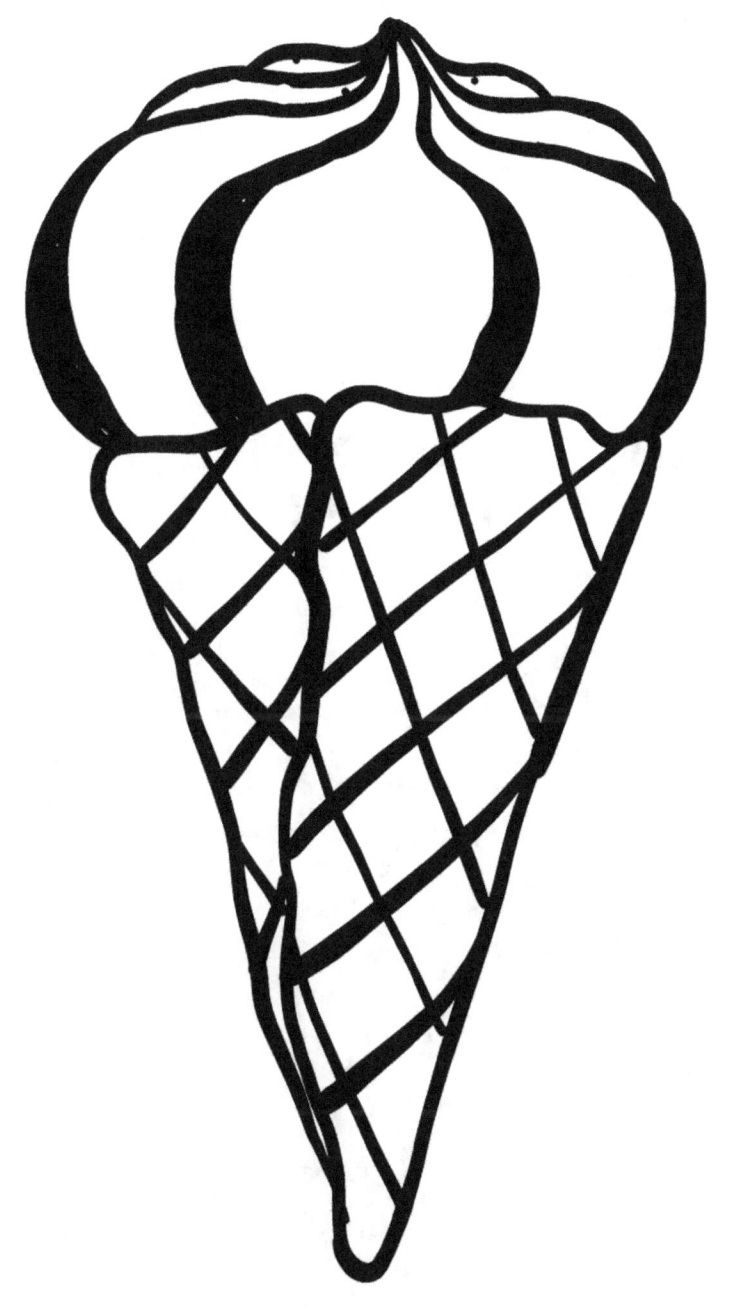

Popsicle

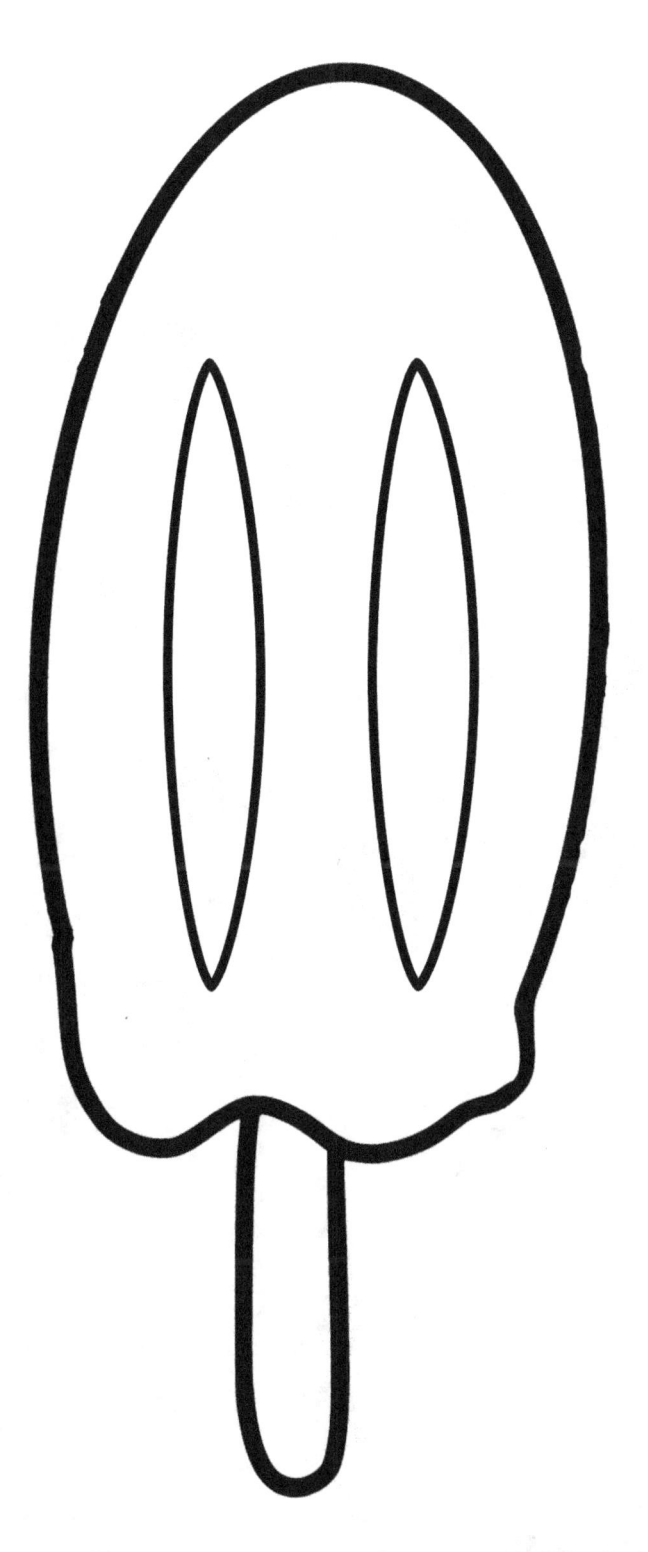

Ice Cream Cone

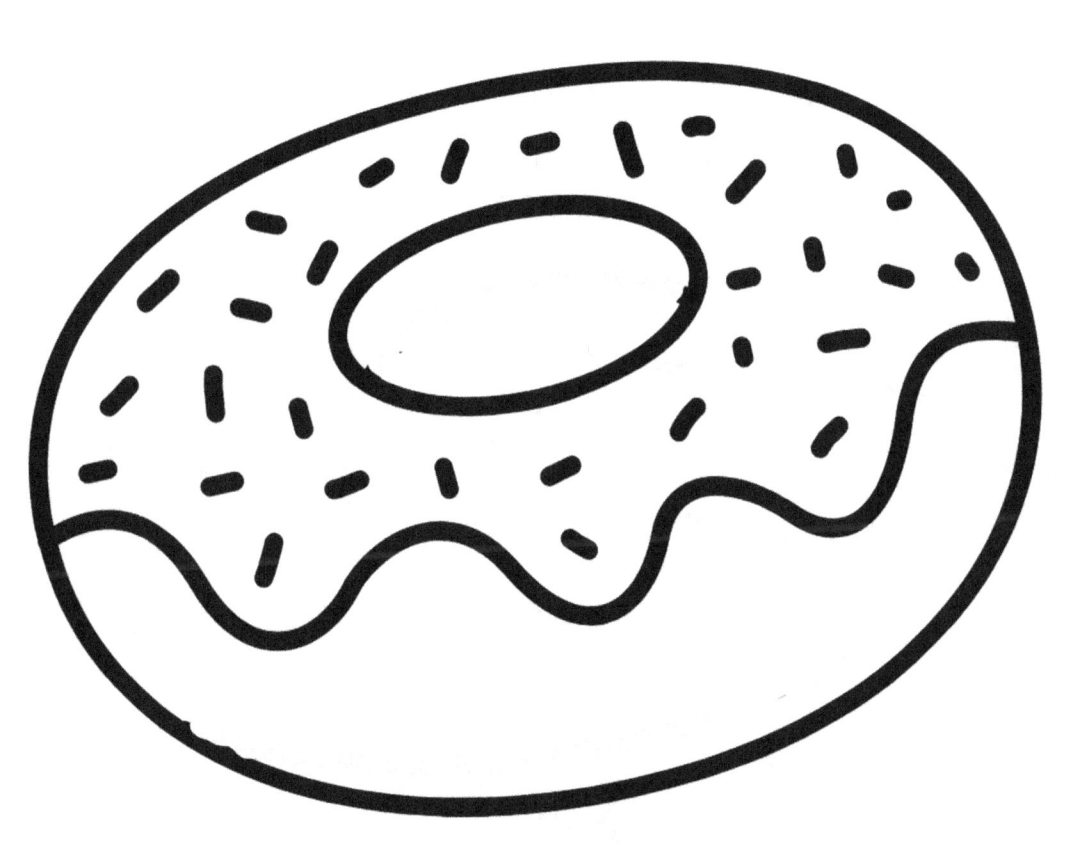

Season Greetings